I0605812

THE LITTLE BOOK OF
PSALMS

First published in 2025 by OH
An Imprint of HEADLINE PUBLISHING GROUP LIMITED

1

Disclaimer:
All trademarks, copyright, quotations, company names, registered names, products, characters, logos and catchphrases used or cited in this book are the property of their respective owners.

Cataloguing in Publication Data is available from the British Library

ISBN 978-1-03543-027-7

Compiled and written by: Stella Caldwell
Editorial: Saneaah Muhammad
Designed and typeset in Palatino Nova Pro by: Andy Jones
Project manager: Russell Porter
Production: Arlene Lestarde
Printed and bound in Dubai

Headline's policy is to use papers that are natural, renewable and recyclable products and made from wood grown in well-managed forests and other controlled sources. The logging and manufacturing processes are expected to conform to the environmental regulations of the country of origin.

HEADLINE PUBLISHING GROUP LIMITED
An Hachette UK Company
Carmelite House, 50 Victoria Embankment, London EC4Y 0DZ

The authorised representative in the EEA is Hachette Ireland, 8 Castlecourt Centre, Dublin 15, D15 XTP3, Ireland (email: info@hbgi.ie)

www.headline.co.uk www.hachette.co.uk

THE LITTLE BOOK OF
PSALMS

WORDS OF PRAISE, COMFORT
AND HOPE

CONTENTS

INTRODUCTION

The Book of Psalms is one of the Bible's most cherished books. A timeless source of inspiration, its words – of praise, comfort, sorrow and hope – have soothed and uplifted hearts for more than 3,000 years.

Written between approximately 1400 BCE and 500 BCE, the Psalms span centuries of Israel's history. They express the deepest human emotions, reminding us of God's presence in every season of life. Whether reflecting times of heartache or joy, these sacred writings continue to resonate with people, offering a voice to the human soul.

The Psalms are songs and prayers that encompass the full range of human experience. They vary in form, from hymns and laments to declarations of praise and thanksgiving. Many were written by King David, a shepherd and ruler whose life was marked by both triumph and failure, yet always by a deep longing for God. Others were composed by Moses, Asaph and the sons of Korah – prophets, priests and musicians who led God's people in worship. Their words have been sung, recited and cherished for millennia.

The Psalms played a central role in ancient temple rituals and continue to shape Christian and Jewish faith today. Their structure is rich with poetic beauty, featuring vivid imagery and heartfelt expression. Some are deeply personal, while others were written for communal worship. They celebrate God's greatness, cry out in desperation, and declare his mercy, justice and love.

Within these pages, you'll find carefully selected verses organized into themes that reflect our relationship with God. Alongside these, historical facts and insights provide a deeper understanding of their significance.

So, read on – and allow these words to uplift your spirit, strengthen your faith and remind you that in every circumstance, God is near.

CHAPTER

PRAISE AND WORSHIP

At the heart of the Psalms is the theme of praise and worship – an invitation to glorify God in every circumstance.

They call believers to seek him in sorrow, exalt him in joy and trust him in every season.

"Blessed is the one who does not walk in step with the wicked or stand in the way that sinners take or sit in the company of mockers, but whose delight is in the law of the Lord, and who meditates on his law day and night."

Psalm 1:1–3

"Rejoice in the Lord and be glad, you righteous; sing, all you who are upright in heart!"

Psalm 32:11

"

Praise the Lord. Praise God in his sanctuary; praise him in his mighty heavens. Praise him for his acts of power; praise him for his surpassing greatness. Praise him with the sounding of the trumpet, praise him with the harp and lyre, praise him with timbrel and dancing, praise him with the strings and pipe, praise him with the clash of cymbals, praise him with resounding cymbals. Let everything that has breath praise the Lord.

"

Psalm 150:1–6

“Shout for joy to the Lord, all the earth, burst into jubilant song with music; make music to the Lord with the harp, with the harp and the sound of singing, with trumpets and the blast of the ram's horn – shout for joy before the Lord, the King.”

Psalm 98:4–6

ith 30,147 words, the Book of Psalms is the third longest book in the Bible – following Jeremiah and Genesis. Containing 2,461 verses, it spans a vast range of human emotions – from joy and thanksgiving to sorrow, repentance and deep longing for God. The Psalms serve as songs, prayers and poems that have remained central to the Jewish and Christian faiths for centuries.

I believe that a man can find nothing more glorious than these Psalms; for they embrace the whole life of man, the affections of his mind and the motions of his soul. To praise and glorify God, he can select a psalm suited to every occasion, and thus will find that they were written for him.

Athanasius (c.296–373),
Bishop of Alexandria

“I will extol the Lord at all times; his praise will always be on my lips. I will glory in the Lord; let the afflicted hear and rejoice. Glorify the Lord with me; let us exalt his name together.”

Psalm 34:1–3

“

Sing joyfully to the Lord, you righteous; it is fitting for the upright to praise him. Praise the Lord with the harp; make music to him on the ten-stringed lyre. Sing to him a new song; play skilfully, and shout for joy.

”

Psalm 33:1–3

Clap your hands, all you nations; shout to God with cries of joy. For the Lord Most High is awesome, the great King over all the earth.

Psalm 47:1–2

"I will be fully satisfied as with the richest of foods; with singing lips my mouth will praise you."

Psalm 63:5

"

Shout for joy to God, all the earth! Sing the glory of his name; make his praise glorious. Say to God, 'How awesome are your deeds! So great is your power that your enemies cringe before you. All the earth bows down to you; they sing praise to you, they sing the praises of your name.'

"

Psalm 66:1–4

“May the nations be glad and sing for joy, for you rule the peoples with equity and guide the nations of the earth.”

Psalm 67:4

"

How lovely is your dwelling place, Lord Almighty! My soul yearns, even faints, for the courts of the Lord; my heart and my flesh cry out for the living God. Even the sparrow has found a home, and the swallow a nest for herself, where she may have her young – a place near your altar, Lord Almighty, my King and my God. Blessed are those who dwell in your house; they are ever praising you.

"

Psalm 84:1–4

“Glory in his holy name; let the hearts of those who seek the Lord rejoice.”

Psalm 105:3

Light shines on the righteous and joy on the upright in heart. Rejoice in the Lord, you who are righteous, and praise his holy name.

Psalm 97:11–12

He put a new song in my mouth, a hymn of praise to our God. Many will see and fear the Lord and put their trust in him.

Psalm 40:3

he Book of Psalms is divided into five sections (Psalms 1–41, 42–72, 73–89, 90–106 and 107–150), mirroring the five books of the Torah (Genesis to Deuteronomy). Each section concludes with a "doxology" – a short hymn of praise signifying the completion of that portion.

"

Hence it is that the Psalter is the Book of all saints; and everyone, in whatever situation he may be, finds in that situation psalms and words that fit his case, that suit him as if they were put there just for his sake, so that he could not put it better himself, or find or wish for anything better.

"

Martin Luther (1483–1546),
German priest and theologian

"Shout for joy to the Lord, all the earth. Worship the Lord with gladness; come before him with joyful songs. Know that the Lord is God. It is he who made us, and we are his; we are his people, the sheep of his pasture."

Psalm 100:1–3

"Our mouths were filled with laughter, our tongues with songs of joy. Then it was said among the nations, 'The Lord has done great things for them.' The Lord has done great things for us, and we are filled with joy."

Psalm 126:2–3

"Sing to the Lord a new song; sing to the Lord, all the earth. Sing to the Lord, praise his name; proclaim his salvation day after day."

Psalm 96:1–2

"I will praise you, Lord, among the nations; I will sing of you among the peoples. For great is your love, higher than the heavens; your faithfulness reaches to the skies. Be exalted, O God, above the heavens; may Your glory cover all the earth."

Psalm 108:3–5

"Praise the Lord, my soul; all my inmost being, praise his holy name."

Psalm 103:1

"I seek you with all my heart; do not let me stray from your commands. I have hidden your word in my heart, that I might not sin against you. Praise be to you, Lord; teach me your decrees. With my lips I recount all the laws that come from your mouth."

Psalm 119:10–13

ing David wrote at least 73 psalms, making him the most prolific psalmist. As a musician and poet, he used the Psalms to express joy, struggles, repentance and devotion to God. Other authors who contributed include Moses, Solomon, Asaph, the Sons of Korah, Ethan and Heman. Some psalms remain anonymous.

What is there necessary for a man to know which the Psalms are not able to teach?

Richard Hooker (1554–1600),
Church of England priest and theologian

“Let them praise his name with dancing and make music to him with timbrel and harp. For the Lord takes delight in his people; he crowns the humble with victory.”

Psalm 149:3

"

My mouth will speak in praise of the Lord. Let every creature praise his holy name for ever and ever.

"

Psalm 145:21

CHAPTER

COMFORT AND SOLACE

In moments of fear, sorrow or uncertainty, the Psalms remind us that God is our rock, our shelter and our ever-present help. They assure us that even in life's darkest valleys, his love sustains, his peace calms and his promises give hope.

"In peace I will lie
down and sleep,
for you alone, Lord,
make me dwell
in safety."

Psalm 4:8

Truly my soul finds rest in God; my salvation comes from him. Truly he is my rock and my salvation; he is my fortress, I will never be shaken.

Psalm 62:1–2

“The Lord is my shepherd, I lack nothing. He makes me lie down in green pastures, he leads me beside quiet waters, he refreshes my soul. He guides me along the right paths for his name's sake. Even though I walk through the darkest valley, I will fear no evil, for you are with me; your rod and your staff, they comfort me.”

Psalm 23:1–4

Surely your goodness and love will follow me all the days of my life, and I will dwell in the house of the Lord forever.

Psalm 23:6

salm 23, attributed to King David, is one of the most famous passages in the Bible. Written around 1000 BCE, it portrays God as a caring shepherd who provides, protects and guides. This was a common idea in ancient times when kings were seen as shepherds of their people.

The most valuable thing the Psalms do for me is to express the same delight in God which made David dance.

C. S. Lewis (1898–1963),
English writer, scholar and theologian

"The Lord is close to the broken-hearted and saves those who are crushed in spirit."

Psalm 34:18

"I waited patiently for the Lord; he turned to me and heard my cry. He lifted me out of the slimy pit, out of the mud and mire; he set my feet on a rock and gave me a firm place to stand."

Psalm 40:1–2

"Be still, and know that I am God."

Psalm 46:10

The Lord Almighty is with us; the God of Jacob is our fortress.

Psalm 46:11

any psalms contain Messianic prophecies, foretelling aspects of Jesus' life, suffering and resurrection. For example, Psalm 22 vividly describes the crucifixion, including Jesus' words on the cross, while Psalm 110 proclaims Christ as the eternal King and Priest.

"

My God, my God, why have you forsaken me? Why are you so far from saving me, so far from my cries of anguish? My God, I cry out by day, but you do not answer, by night, but I find no rest. Yet you are enthroned as the Holy One; you are the one Israel praises. In you our ancestors put their trust; they trusted and you delivered them.

"

Psalm 22:1–4

"Praise be to the Lord, to God our Saviour, who daily bears our burdens."

Psalm 68:19

"The Lord is a refuge for the oppressed, a stronghold in times of trouble. Those who know your name trust in you, for you, Lord, have never forsaken those who seek you."

Psalm 9:9–10

"Hear my cry, O God; listen to my prayer. From the ends of the earth I call to you, I call as my heart grows faint; lead me to the rock that is higher than I. For you have been my refuge, a strong tower against the foe."

Psalm 61:1–3

"You, Lord, are forgiving and good, abounding in love to all who call to you. Hear my prayer, Lord; listen to my cry for mercy. When I am in distress, I call to you, because you answer me."

Psalm 86:5–7

he Psalms were originally sung or chanted in the Jewish Temple as part of worship, often led by Levite musicians. Many were accompanied by instruments such as harps, lyres, cymbals and trumpets, creating a rich musical tradition.

"*The Book of Psalms is a compend of all divinity; a common store of medicine for the soul; a universal magazine of good doctrines profitable to everyone in all conditions.*"

Basil the Great (c.330–79),
Bishop of Caesarea

"When I said,
'My foot is slipping',
your unfailing love,
Lord, supported me.
When anxiety was
great within me, your
consolation brought
me joy."

Psalm 94:18–19

But as for me, it is good to be near God. I have made the Sovereign Lord my refuge; I will tell of all your deeds.

Psalm 73:28

“Whoever dwells in the shelter of the Most High will rest in the shadow of the Almighty. I will say of the Lord, ‘He is my refuge and my fortress, my God, in whom I trust.’”

Psalm 91:1–2

Lord, you alone are
my portion and my
cup; you make my
lot secure.

Psalm 16:5

"For his anger lasts only a moment, but his favour lasts a lifetime; weeping may stay for the night, but rejoicing comes in the morning."

Psalm 30:5

For in the day of trouble he will keep me safe in his dwelling; he will hide me in the shelter of his sacred tent and set me high upon a rock.

Psalm 27:5

CHAPTER

STRENGTH AND COURAGE

The Psalms are a wellspring of strength, renewing weary souls and fortifying hearts in times of trial. In the face of fear, adversity or the unknown, they remind us that God goes before us – upholding, guiding and filling us with the courage to press on.

"I lift up my eyes to the hills. From where does my help come? My help comes from the Lord, the Maker of heaven and earth. He will not allow your foot to slip; your Protector will not slumber. Behold, the Protector of Israel will neither slumber nor sleep."

Psalm 121:1–4

But you, Lord, are a shield around me, my glory, the One who lifts my head high.

”

Psalm 3:3

"Be strong and take heart, all you who hope in the Lord."

Psalm 31:24

For You, O Lord, light my lamp; my God lights up my darkness.

”

Psalm 18:28

Psalm 90, attributed to Moses, is considered the oldest psalm. If it does indeed date back to Moses' time, it would have been written around 1400–1200 BCE, during Israel's wilderness period. This psalm reflects on human frailty, God's eternity and the need for divine guidance and mercy.

"

Lord, you have been our dwelling place throughout all generations. Before the mountains were born or you brought forth the whole world, from everlasting to everlasting, you are God.

"

Psalm 90:1–2

"

The Lord is my light and my salvation – whom shall I fear? The Lord is the stronghold of my life – of whom shall I be afraid?

"

Psalm 27:1

"Let the morning bring me
word of your unfailing love,
for I have put my trust in you.
Show me the way I should go,
for to you I entrust
my life."

Psalm 143:8

In you, Lord, I have taken refuge;
let me never be put to shame;
deliver me in your righteousness.
Turn your ear to me, come quickly
to my rescue; be my rock of refuge,
a strong fortress to save me. Since
you are my rock and my fortress,
for the sake of your name lead
and guide me.

Psalm 31:1–3

“The Lord is my rock, my fortress and my deliverer; my God is my rock, in whom I take refuge, my shield and the horn of my salvation, my stronghold.”

Psalm 18:2

"The salvation of the righteous comes from the Lord; he is their stronghold in time of trouble. The Lord helps them and delivers them; he delivers them from the wicked and saves them, because they take refuge in him."

Psalm 37:39–40

"I sought the Lord, and he answered me; he delivered me from all my fears."

Psalm 34:4

The Psalms in Numbers

19th book in the Bible
150 chapters
2,461 verses
43,743 words

"

Nowhere have I found words more powerful than those in the Psalms. Their fervid poetry cleanses one, gives one strength, brings hope in moments of darkness. Makes one look critically into oneself, convict oneself, and wash one's heart clean with one's own tears. It is the ever-burning fire of love, of gratitude, humility and truth.

"

Svetlana Alliluyeva (1926–2011), the only daughter of Josef Stalin. In 1967, she defected from Russia to the US where she converted to the Catholic faith.

"The Lord makes firm the steps of the one who delights in him; though he may stumble, he will not fall, for the Lord upholds him with his hand."

Psalm 37:23–24

“

God is our refuge and strength,
an ever-present help in trouble.
Therefore we will not fear, though
the earth give way and the
mountains fall into the heart of
the sea, though its waters roar and
foam and the mountains quake
with their surging.

”

Psalm 46:1–3

"As for me, I call to God, and the Lord saves me. Evening, morning, and noon I cry out in distress, and he hears my voice."

Psalm 55:16–17

"Cast your cares on the Lord and he will sustain you; he will never let the righteous be shaken."

Psalm 55:22

salm 119 is the longest chapter in the Bible, with 176 verses. Structured as an acrostic poem based on the Hebrew alphabet, it emphasizes devotion to God's law – using repeated words such as "statutes", "commandments" and "precepts". The author is unknown, though David, Ezra or Daniel have been suggested as possible writers.

“

Your word is a lamp to my feet and a light to my path.

”

Psalm 119:105

"Yes, my soul, find rest in God; hope comes from him. Truly he is my rock and my salvation; he is my fortress, I will not be shaken. My salvation and my honour depend on God; he is my mighty rock, my refuge. Trust in him at all times, you people; pour out your hearts to him, for God is our refuge."

Psalm 62:5–8

"When I am afraid, I put my trust in you. In God, whose word I praise – in God I trust and am not afraid. What can mere mortals do to me?"

Psalm 56:3–4

“For you have been my hope, Sovereign Lord, my confidence since my youth. From birth I have relied on you; you brought me forth from my mother's womb. I will ever praise you. I have become a sign to many; you are my strong refuge. My mouth is filled with your praise, declaring your splendour all day long.”

Psalm 71:5–8

He heals the brokenhearted and binds up their wounds. He determines the number of the stars and calls them each by name. Great is our Lord and mighty in power; his understanding has no limit. The Lord sustains the humble but casts the wicked to the ground.

Psalm 147:3–6

salms Authors

73 (almost half) by King David

12 by Asaph (50, 73–83)

10 by the sons of Korah (42, 44, 45, 46, 47, 48, 49,84, 85, 87)

2 by Solomon (2 and 127)

1 by Moses (90)

1 by Herman (88)

1 by Ethan (89)

50 anonymous

I will sing of the Lord's great love forever; with my mouth I will make your faithfulness known through all generations. I will declare that your love stands firm forever, that you have established your faithfulness in heaven itself.

Psalm 89:1–2

"My flesh and my heart may fail, but God is the strength of my heart and my portion forever."

Psalm 73:26

If I go up to the heavens, you are there; if I make my bed in the depths, you are there. If I rise on the wings of the dawn, if I settle on the far side of the sea, even there your hand will guide me, your right hand will hold me fast.

”

Psalm 139:8–10

The Lord is my strength and my shield; my heart trusts in him, and he helps me. My heart leaps for joy, and with my song I praise him.

Psalm 28:7

The Lord upholds all who fall and lifts up all who are bowed down.

Psalm 145:14

CHAPTER 4

FAITH AND HOPE

Echoing with unwavering hope, the Psalms remind us that trust in the Lord is never in vain. Through every storm and sorrow, they assure us that God is our refuge, our strength and the rock on which we stand.

"In you, Lord my God, I put my trust. I trust in you; do not let me be put to shame, nor let my enemies triumph over me."

Psalm 25:1–2

I keep my eyes always on the Lord. With him at my right hand, I will not be shaken.

”

Psalm 16:8

"May he give you the desire of your heart and make all your plans succeed. May we shout for joy over your victory and lift up our banners in the name of our God."

Psalm 20:4–5

Show me your ways, Lord, teach me your paths. Guide me in your truth and teach me, for you are God my Saviour, and my hope is in you all day long.

”

Psalm 25:4–5

he Book of Psalms is often called "Tehillim", meaning "Praises". It is also referred to as the "Bible within the Bible" since it covers major biblical themes, such as creation, sin, redemption and God's faithfulness.

The Psalms are a Little Bible, wherein everything contained in the entire Bible is beautifully and briefly comprehended.

Martin Luther (1483–1546),
German priest and theologian

“

I will praise you, Lord, with all my heart; before the 'gods' I will sing your praise. I will bow down toward your holy temple and will praise your name for your unfailing love and your faithfulness, for you have so exalted your solemn decree that it surpasses your fame. When I called, you answered me; you greatly emboldened me.

”

Psalm 138:1–3

As for me, I will always have hope; I will praise you more and more.

”

Psalm 71:14

"Commit your way to the Lord; trust in him and he will do this: He will make your righteous reward shine like the dawn, your vindication like the noonday sun."

Psalm 37: 5–6

Blessed is the one who trusts in the Lord, who does not look to the proud, to those who turn aside to false gods.

Psalm 40:4

I remain confident of this: I will see the goodness of the Lord in the land of the living. Wait for the Lord; be strong and take heart and wait for the Lord.

Psalm 27:13–14

But the eyes of the Lord are on those who fear him, on those whose hope is in his unfailing love.

Psalm 33:18

Why, my soul, are you downcast? Why so disturbed within me? Put your hope in God, for I will yet praise him, my Saviour and my God.

”

Psalm 42:5

“

Do not fret because of those who are evil or be envious of those who do wrong; for like the grass they will soon wither, like green plants they will soon die away. Trust in the Lord and do good; dwell in the land and enjoy safe pasture. Take delight in the Lord, and he will give you the desires of your heart.

”

Psalm 37:1–4

n extra psalm, Psalm 151, is found in the *Septuagint* (the Greek translation of the Old Testament) and the Dead Sea Scrolls. Said to be written by King David after he slew Goliath, it reflects on his humble beginnings as a shepherd and his divine selection to be Israel's king.

“

I was small among my brothers, and the youngest in my father's house; I tended my father's sheep.

”

Psalm 151,
attributed to King David,
from the *Septuagint*

He will cover you with his feathers, and under his wings you will find refuge; his faithfulness will be your shield and rampart.

Psalm 91:4

Be still before the Lord
and wait patiently for him;
do not fret when people
succeed in their ways,
when they carry out their
wicked schemes.

Psalm 37:7

“

But I am like an olive tree
flourishing in the house of God;
I trust in God's unfailing love for
ever and ever. For what you have
done I will always praise you in the
presence of your faithful people.
And I will hope in your name, for
your name is good.

”

Psalm 52:8–9

Turn from evil and do good; then you will dwell in the land forever. For the Lord loves the just and will not forsake his faithful ones.

Psalm 37:27–28

For the Lord God is a sun and shield; the Lord bestows favour and honour; no good thing does he withhold from those whose walk is blameless.

Psalm 84:11

But now, Lord, what do I look for? My hope is in you.

Psalm 39:7

"You will not fear the terror of night, nor the arrow that flies by day, nor the pestilence that stalks in the darkness, nor the plague that destroys at midday. A thousand may fall at your side, ten thousand at your right hand, but it will not come near you."

Psalm 91:5–7

But I trust in you, Lord; I say, 'You are my God'. My times are in your hands; deliver me from the hands of my enemies, from those who pursue me.

Psalm 31:14–15

salm 117 – author unknown – is the shortest psalm and the shortest chapter in the entire Bible. It consists of only two verses, but despite its brevity, it delivers a powerful message, calling all nations and people to praise God.

Praise the Lord, all you nations; extol him, all you peoples. For great is his love toward us, and the faithfulness of the Lord endures forever. Praise the Lord.

Psalm 117

May the Lord cause you to flourish, both you and your children. May you be blessed by the Lord, the Maker of heaven and earth.

Psalm 115:14–15

You are my refuge and my shield; I have put my hope in your word.

”

Psalm 119:114

Blessed are those whose help is the God of Jacob, whose hope is in the Lord their God.

Psalm 146:5

"I wait for the Lord, my whole being waits, and in his word I put my hope. I wait for the Lord more than watchmen wait for the morning, more than watchmen wait for the morning."

Psalm 130:5–6

"Surely the righteous will never be shaken; they will be remembered forever. They will have no fear of bad news; their hearts are steadfast, trusting in the Lord."

Psalm 112:6–7

Come and see what the Lord has done, the desolations he has brought on the earth. He makes wars cease to the ends of the earth. He breaks the bow and shatters the spear; he burns the shields with fire.

Psalm 46:8–9

CHAPTER 5

REPENTANCE AND RENEWAL

The Psalms encourage us to turn from our failures and seek God's healing grace. They guide us from brokenness to restoration, reminding us that his love renews and strengthens all who come to him with humility and faith.

Have mercy on me, O God, according to your unfailing love; according to your great compassion blot out my transgressions. Wash away all my iniquity and cleanse me from my sin.

”

Psalm 51:1–2

“Create in me a pure heart, O
God, and renew a steadfast spirit
within me. Do not cast me from
your presence or take your Holy
Spirit from me. Restore to me
the joy of your salvation
and grant me a willing spirit,
to sustain me.”

Psalm 51:10–12

“Then I acknowledged my sin to you and did not cover up my iniquity. I said, 'I will confess my transgressions to the Lord.' And you forgave the guilt of my sin.”

Psalm 32:5

Lord, do not forsake me; do not be far from me, my God. Come quickly to help me, my Lord and my Saviour.

”

Psalm 38:21–22

he name YHWH (Yahweh), meaning "Lord", appears over 600 times in the Book of Psalms, making it the most frequently used word. "Elohim" ("God") is also common but occurs less often than "Lord". Other powerful words that appear throughout the Psalms include "praise", "mercy", "righteousness" and "heart".

Lord, you are the God who saves me; day and night I cry out to you. May my prayer come before you; turn your ear to my cry.

”

Psalm 88:1–2

“Out of the depths I cry to you, Lord; Lord, hear my voice. Let your ears be attentive to my cry for mercy. If you, Lord, kept a record of sins, Lord, who could stand? But with you there is forgiveness, so that we can, with reverence, serve you.”

Psalm 130:1–4

“

Good and upright is the Lord; therefore he instructs sinners in his ways. He guides the humble in what is right and teaches them his way. All the ways of the Lord are loving and faithful toward those who keep the demands of his covenant. For the sake of your name, Lord, forgive my iniquity, though it is great.

”

Psalm 25:8–11

"You, God, know my folly;
my guilt is not hidden
from you."

Psalm 69:5

“Lord, hear my prayer, listen to my cry for mercy; in your faithfulness and righteousness come to my relief.”

Psalm 143:1

You, God, are my God, earnestly I seek you; I thirst for you, my whole being longs for you, in a dry and parched land where there is no water.

Psalm 63:1

“

On my bed I remember you;
I think of you through the
watches of the night. Because
you are my help, I sing in the
shadow of your wings.
I cling to you; your right
hand upholds me.

”

Psalm 63:6–8

The Lord is compassionate and gracious, slow to anger, abounding in love. He will not always accuse, nor will he harbour his anger forever; he does not treat us as our sins deserve or repay us according to our iniquities.

Psalm 103:8–11

> "You turned my wailing into dancing; you removed my sackcloth and clothed me with joy, that my heart may sing your praises and not be silent. Lord my God, I will praise you forever."

Psalm 30:11–12

he word "Selah" appears 71 times in the Book of Psalms and three times in the Book of Habakkuk. Its exact meaning is unknown, but scholars suggest it could signify a musical pause, a call to reflect, or a form of emphasis – a bit like "Amen".

They have sharpened their tongues like a serpent; adders' poison is under their lips. Selah.

Psalm 140:3
(King James Version)

"Restore us again, God our Saviour, and put away your displeasure toward us."

Psalm 85:4

“

Remember your word to your servant, for you have given me hope. My comfort in my suffering is this: Your promise preserves my life.

”

Psalm 119:49–50

“

Blessed is the one whose
transgressions are forgiven,
whose sins are covered.
Blessed is the one whose
sin the Lord does not count
against them and in whose
spirit is no deceit.

”

Psalm 32:1–2

"

Hear me, Lord, and answer me, for I am poor and needy. Guard my life, for I am faithful to you; save your servant who trusts in you. You are my God; have mercy on me, Lord, for I call to you all day long. Bring joy to your servant, Lord, for I put my trust in you.

"

Psalm 86:1–4

"Do not remember the sins of my youth and my rebellious ways; according to your love remember me, for you, Lord, are good."

Psalm 25:7

“The life of mortals is like grass, they flourish like a flower of the field; the wind blows over it and it is gone, and its place remembers it no more. But from everlasting to everlasting the Lord’s love is with those who fear him, and his righteousness with their children’s children – with those who keep his covenant and remember to obey his precepts.”

Psalm 103:15–18

he Songs of Ascents are a collection of 15 psalms (Psalms 120–134), traditionally sung by Jewish pilgrims as they travelled to Jerusalem for festivals like Passover, Pentecost and Tabernacles. These psalms express both the physical and spiritual journey toward God, and include verses such as "I lift up my eyes to the hills" (Psalm 121) and "I was glad when they said unto me" (Psalm 122).

“

The more deeply we grow into the psalms and the more often we pray them as our own, the simpler and richer will our prayer become.

Dietrich Bonhoeffer (1906–45),
German Lutheran pastor and theologian

“Cleanse me with hyssop, and I will be clean; wash me, and I will be whiter than snow. Let me hear joy and gladness; let the bones you have crushed rejoice. Hide your face from my sins and blot out all my iniquity.”

Psalm 51:7–9

"But You, O Lord, are a compassionate and gracious God, slow to anger, abounding in loving devotion and faithfulness."

Psalm 86:15

As far as the east is from the west, so far has he removed our transgressions from us.

”

Psalm 103:12

For your name's sake, Lord, preserve my life; in your righteousness, bring me out of trouble.

Psalm 143:11

CHAPTER 6

LOVE AND GRATITUDE

In times of joy and sorrow, the Psalms teach us to trust in God's goodness and give thanks for his faithfulness. Through praise and prayer, they remind us that God's love sustains, comforts and renews our souls.

"

I love the Lord, for he heard my voice; he heard my cry for mercy. Because he turned his ear to me, I will call on him as long as I live.

"

Psalm 116:1–2

For the word of the Lord is right and true; he is faithful in all he does. The Lord loves righteousness and justice; the earth is full of his unfailing love.

”

Psalm 33:4–5

"I will give thanks to you, Lord, with all my heart; I will tell of all your wonderful deeds. I will be glad and rejoice in you; I will sing the praises of your name, O Most High."

Psalm 9:1

But I trust in your unfailing love; my heart rejoices in your salvation. I will sing the Lord's praise, for he has been good to me.

”

Psalm 13:5–6

lmost half of the direct quotes from the Old Testament found in the New Testament come from the Psalms. This book is frequently referenced, appearing 103 times in the book of Revelation and 149 times across the four Gospels, either through direct quotations or allusions.

All the wonders of Greek civilization heaped together are less wonderful than is the single Book of Psalms…

”

William Gladstone (1809–98), British prime minister

"I will be glad and rejoice in your love, for you saw my affliction and knew the anguish of my soul. You have not given me into the hands of the enemy but have set my feet in a spacious place."

Psalm 31:7–8

“For you, Lord, have delivered me from death, my eyes from tears, my feet from stumbling, that I may walk before the Lord in the land of the living.”

Psalm 116:8–9

"How priceless is your unfailing love, O God! People take refuge in the shadow of your wings. They feast on the abundance of your house; you give them drink from your river of delights. For with you is the fountain of life; in your light we see light."

Psalm 36:7–9

Many, Lord my God, are the wonders you have done, the things you planned for us. None can compare with you; were I to speak and tell of your deeds, they would be too many to declare.

”

Psalm 40:5

“By day the Lord directs his love, at night his song is with me – a prayer to the God of my life.”

Psalm 42:8

Within your temple, O God, we meditate on your unfailing love.

”

Psalm 48:9

salm 118 is considered the central chapter of the Bible. Interestingly, the centre of that psalm – 118:8 – states, "It is better to take refuge in the Lord than to trust in man."

For 3,000 years they have been the highest manual of devotion among men. Nothing like them can be found in all antiquity! Greece has spoken! Rome has had the ear of the ages! Modern time has uttered all its voices: but the Psalms remain wholly unsurpassed!

Dr Joseph Cook (1838–1901),
American philosophical lecturer,
clergyman and writer

“

It is good to praise the Lord and make music to your name, O Most High, proclaiming your love in the morning and your faithfulness at night.

”

Psalm 92:1–2

Give thanks to the Lord, for he is good; his love endures forever.

Psalm 118:1

"

I will praise God's name in song and glorify him with thanksgiving. This will please the Lord more than an ox, more than a bull with its horns and hooves.

"

Psalm 69:30–31

I will praise you, Lord, among the nations; I will sing of you among the peoples. For great is your love, reaching to the heavens; your faithfulness reaches to the skies.

Psalm 57:9–10

"Come, let us sing for joy to the Lord; let us shout aloud to the Rock of our salvation. Let us come before him with thanksgiving and extol him with music and song. For the Lord is the great God, the great King above all gods."

Psalm 95:1–3

"You have searched me, Lord, and you know me. You know when I sit and when I rise; you perceive my thoughts from afar. You discern my going out and my lying down; you are familiar with all my ways."

Psalm 139:1–3

"I put no trust in my bow,
my sword does not bring
me victory; but you give us
victory over our enemies, you
put our adversaries to shame.
In God we make our boast all
day long, and we will praise
your name forever."

Psalm 44:6–8

“

Praise the Lord, my soul, and forget not all his benefits – who forgives all your sins and heals all your diseases, who redeems your life from the pit and crowns you with love and compassion, who satisfies your desires with good things so that your youth is renewed like the eagle's.

”

Psalm 103:2–5

"Praise the Lord. Give thanks to the Lord, for he is good; his love endures forever."

Psalm 106:1

Because your love is better than life, my lips will glorify you. I will praise you as long as I live, and in your name I will lift up my hands.

Psalm 63:3–4

ome psalms follow an acrostic structure, where each section begins with a consecutive letter of the Hebrew alphabet. This poetic device made memorization easier in ancient times. As well as Psalm 119, Psalms 25, 34 and 145 also use this pattern.

The Lord is righteous in all his ways and faithful in all he does. The Lord is near to all who call on him, to all who call on him in truth. He fulfils the desires of those who fear him; he hears their cry and saves them.

Psalm 145:17–19

Give thanks to the Lord, for he is good; his love endures forever. Let the redeemed of the Lord tell their story – those he redeemed from the hand of the foe, those he gathered from the lands, from east and west, from north and south.

Psalm 107:1–3

“For you make me glad by your deeds, Lord; I sing for joy at what your hands have done. How great are your works, Lord, how profound your thoughts!”

Psalm 92:4–5

"Praise the Lord. I will extol the Lord with all my heart in the council of the upright and in the assembly. Great are the works of the Lord; they are pondered by all who delight in them. Glorious and majestic are his deeds, and his righteousness endures forever."

Psalm 111:1–3

Sacrifice thank offerings to God, fulfil your vows to the Most High, and call on me in the day of trouble; I will deliver you, and you will honour me.

Psalm 50:14–15

Enter his gates with thanksgiving and his courts with praise; give thanks to him and praise his name. For the Lord is good and his love endures forever; his faithfulness continues through all generations.

Psalm 100:4–5